Damaged Doesn't Mean Dead

Poetry by

Shaun Payton

Cover art creative attribution to
www.CoverDesignStudio.com and Gabor Dvornik

For everyone who has
Inspired me to write.

Damaged Doesn't Mean Dead

"there's a bluebird in my heart that wants to get out, but I'm too tough for him." Charles Bukowski, the bluebird

The Murderer

The murderer is hard, convinced.
The substance of self assumes the position.
and there are others.
We look at each other, "Are you dead too?"
looking into the palms of our hands, whose
body have we touched? whose mind have we
ravaged? why is time not a registering notion?

I dreamed, like a rat in a maze, unwavering
confused, determined and undermined
it was the first sweat I broke, clever drops
of distinction marked where I had awoken.

The murderer is true, the weight of confessions
bows the head, fuck, there is no mercy.
others are running, we share the same feet
like chickens without heads, voices without depth
reasons without thoughts, we choke on this created
thing, tie the laces and kick the chair out.

All this work to discover nowhere was home all along
has blessed sight worth its salt, we are our own murderer
when through no matter what, we are willing to be the rat

Light On a Stranger

Light on a stranger is revealing
Whether it's their secret wisdoms
in their wrinkles or the vanity of
surgery,
There are reasons why people are
who they are,
Wars have hardened them, broken
their chest open, ripped out things
we could never pick up again.
Should it be yours or mine to judge
what the light reveals with repugnance?
Or is it pity? What do we do with the it?
What say you of your own struggles?
Your own self-deceiving yourself
out of its shadow, you'd stomp its
head, riddling yourself with clueless
intentions.
We can hear the squawking flying around
from stares of ignorance to voices of
arrogance, and the shit falls at the same
velocity,
I never know who is right or wrong,
Only people have their unreasoning
when light on a stranger is revealing them.

Calling into The Night

The blood of resolve spills over
The illusion was never swallowed
We were only dreaming from the
mouth of emotions calling into the night.

From the tombs of today, tomorrow's
tears of those spirits will stain an hour glass,
They're pounding on the resistance, struggling
pleas calling into the night.

Fear studying the aura of hearts, deep true
intentions of good and evil stripe deception.
There is more clutching with desperation
when your breath is choked from calling
into the apparition that is the night.

A safe surrender? A concession to please?
We will not dive and dig for the pennies
This is the blood of the living, the sacrifice
of ancestors left in books when their voices
are calling into the night, "The blood of resolve
spills over."

Die Poetry

Die poetry;
As soundless as evaporation;
Won't you grant me this wish?
You lick my eyes and chap
the lips of my soul.

Die poetry;
my heart will not mend
two stanzas more, this
thickness comes quickly
to bury me in its grave.

Die poetry;
My dying love is on her cross
And helplessly I'm writing
thinned and worn out,

Damn you, die poetry
As my pen weeps, praying
she will breathe each day.

The Plastic People

Plastic men, they must be?
Unstimulated by poverty
Ungoverned by man's decency
Plastic men counting property
Rich in forms and ways
Since greed's infancy.

Yes, they are plastic men
Smoking pipes exhaling critiques
On life and how to live
Those plastic men, what do they give?
But also, the plastic women
By their sides shaving points.

And we the living low
And we the living high
And we the in between
Know luxury to be a cool day
A joyful child's spirit, infectious
Precious, and leaves change and fall
All around the plastic people.

My elastic heart however,
Embraces everything, for unchanging
Would be ignorant of those leaves
As a lonely child grieves
For lost imagination

And we the barely getting by
And we the better off than some
And those elders, and those shelters,
Surely volunteers are not plastic recycled?
I replied, I'd eat hot or cold to suffice
Their welcomed sacrifice

Yes, plastic people they are
With no heart nor spirit

No truer inspiring's, just
two lumps of coal with their tea
And a Hatter who has lost his spunk.

If you care not for others
You, naysayer may be, a plastic being
in no better a doll house than I
But with plays and songs about lovers
I find hope is tied to a moon tide
And the waves crash all around
Those plastic beings.

Grieving boy approaches me
Holding a seashell, he listens to the sea
Though there's none I can see.
He says, 'Sir you have quite the imagination'

I know he is plastic
And I wrap him in paper
tuck him in a box, I smile and say,

'Thank you ma'am, have a nice day'
She smiles not, she's a plastic being,
Sized by cold heart, who killed her wonders?

They are the plastic people
Beings for themselves
Kept within bitter bindings
Placed on shelves
But still I hear my plastic boy,
You have quite the imagination.

These Things

These things were thought to be dead.
How they surface through the decay
to discover life again; such as your eyes
closed and silent.

The mind recalls what crawls
around, like secrets kept, weeping
in the night's illusion of dark security.

O the heart treasures what you used to be,
In the grasp of madness enduring this endless
hallucination of your fingers retreating to their grave.

The Kiss of Tenderness

He finds a broken mask
Stained by tears, he imagines
life again picking it up
and placing it over his face…
The whispering of the heart
"Lover, what wars have you endured?"
the kiss of tragedy tenderly sad
strolling down the looking glass.

'If you're the moon, then what am I?'
"The universe which allows me to exist.
I've walked a thousand times into the quick sands
to feel the pace of breath over take the sounds
of the waves."

'Lover, what pains have you consumed for this?'
"If I am the moon, you are the universe which resonates
in my heart."

When the world sees more than its history and ailments
it discovers the colors of imagination and inspiration again

What can never truly hide our emotions
twisting or burning, time will not carry ages
without warrant.

'If you're the moon, then what am I?'
"You are the universe which allows me to exist
as I am, within the temple of longing."
Some eyes see the hell, some hearts feel heaven
most know both…

Tell me nothing more than, you'll be the universe.

We've Yet to Solve the Light

Will it end the victory lead wounds?
Could you wire the soul to methodology?
Can it break the will and part
the seas? You are crashing
against everyone on fire.
May it be a secret key to freedom?
We've yet to solve the light
when we continue to be covered
by the darkness.
Will it be solvent and pure?
Feel like a newborns innocence
discovering little things.
Within every human being is
the ability to sacrifice and quilt
a warm womb.
It carries no burden,
But can hit you between
the eyes,
it will break you
if you are wiser in ignorance.

He'll Want Your Oceans

Sad, yet deeply beautiful eyes
the broken soul will kiss again
the dews of heart beats drippings.

Time is a cliché - you will soar again
for the symphony of loves sea
crashes against the shore

and the right one will want those waves;
your mind
your sentiments
your soul
your dreams
your body

and he'll want them relentlessly
overflowing.

To No Ends

Her eyes can convince me of anything.
Her body can tell me my hands are crafting
curves to no ends.
Her mind can tell me the shade is the sun
And I would believe it cause I'm warm inside her
pounding away for some truth in the ecstasy,
giving dead things life, making ghost come out
to fuck.

There Will Be

Two awful lovers this year.
A bounced check.
A Utility shut off.
Too many work hours.
Not enough work hours.
So little dreams, wet
Or otherwise.
There will be pretty
women in bikinis
playing volleyball on
the beach. Fine tuned
And not for you to taste.
There will be four seasons
Each with their innocence
And displeasure.
There will be rains and floods
Wildfires or nothing at all.
A few drinks with some friends.
A few arguments with the wife
or future ex.
A couple kissing strangers to
be envious of, they seem happy
as the shadows dance towards the
fading twilight.
There will be a hundred missed calls
And more unreturned.
Bill collectors, goals, and shame.
But on the bright side you are
adaptable, you've come this far.

Kingdom of His Soul

He shall begin with this page
the twisting turmoil of pain
or the mountain tops of highs
with ever lovely snow caps.

The kingdom of his soul
shall remain solid through
though the shadowed death
points its grisly finger
he shall look no further
than the blazing sun.

A heart which aches pulses stronger
in the vivid light he sees out of a pinhole
the desire of his lifetime, a heart hungers more!

It takes and holds like moon to sky
one star out of infinite births
from these roots of earth to the
passions within him never faltering
Though with weighted faults himself
love anchors his will, never quenched
by the poems he writes.

If one tear shall fall it will mark a flow
of overwhelming joys, one-star out
of infinite births, takes and holds
like moon to sky

Ghost in The Room

Come slowly
go quickly.

This doesn't hurt
yet it all aches.
Maybe we've bled
too much where no
one won.

What substance is within death?

Go slowly.
Come quickly.

Artifacts mentally developed
it's nearly always you liquored up
and staring back into the labors
of my mind.

You are the ghost in the room
shivering in the rear view mirror.
Can you not see how hard this is?
Beyond the unperceived lays you
penetrating impervious walls.

You are the ghost in the room
I beg you, come quickly
and go slowly.

Your Touch

I felt your fingers
explore my spirit

and the echoes
of sensations

still remain.

You stole my heart,

from the start

I chose to live
for you

and your touch

still echoes through

my soul.

Again

How sad this shade of blue.
I quit and begin again.
I end and stretch further.

How lonely this hue of remorse.
I forgive and sin again.
I tear and spread wider.

How sweetly this tender melancholy
gnaws on my heart with delicate definition's,
in defeat, I know myself again.

Waking Up Alive

Dark dreams, lucid tears
wiped sanity clear of any trace.
Her deafening screams breaking
stitches at the seams.

Taking place in a flower garden
she is thin and frail, denied
her wings to fly away.

The warden here is a crime, planting
his seed inside her mind
thorns prick at her eyes
such desperate lonely cries.

Vague senses of my compassion's
she's abused held by mental handcuffs
which lock her freedoms inside of her fear.

I can never tell how she survives
for hell does not redeem her
to run through the reigns of fire.

I'm waking up alive, still feeling
her pumping heart to no comfort
all she does is admire this flower garden
where she believes no harm will come.

Heart Strokes

Heat stroked kisses.
Hold me lovers blessing
whisper into me
the sweet salvation
of your breathing.
Touch with the compulsion
of life's interpretations.
I'll pour love into your wounds
until they scar, and should they
peel I will pour more of myself
into you, until I am depleted
and returned by love.
Your heart strokes, heart strokes
leaving wakes across my soul

Stargazer

I will burnout – illuminations
saving grace is an eclipse
of the moon.
The afterglow will be the effigy
of my heart, the moon clinging
to the sky.
I am but a stargazer, adoring;

eclipses of the sun
a rainbow in the dark
tears of sovereign joys.

Her heavenly starlight reigns
as the source of my being
longing to caress the shine,
kissing me out of my dreams
into the universe of her womb.

I am but a stargazer
sitting on the moon
among greater constellations
reaching for the heavenly starlight.

To The Devils Chagrin

Have you seen the weeping willows falling from my eyes?
When you've painted clouds over illusions blue sky
you heard the cracking and left it broken,

to the devils chagrin He's laughing in disbelief.

The armor that has fallen lays claim to defenses
when feeling is natural, conducive electricity
flows through the heart,

to the devils chagrin he's losing time in this prison.

Have you studied the victory in defeat? Some were
marginal in error, some were in the feet and hands
and from mouths born out of the devils' breath.

There were namely concussions to the heat of the
exchange, I spit up teeth and looked at that fool

"You can keep coming Lucifer, for all I am will
walk through every blow."

Some senses went askew, different views were
manipulated to divisions of hearts gone dark
and minds gone sinister,

they drop the ball with the intent to scar something

but to the devils chagrin we wake up in the morning

and I love the sound of her eyes opening.

Seems So Far

I think opening my eyes breaks the sky.
The kid without mercy, the face of nothing
razor sharp, running on glass.

The pale complexions shape shifting
Seems so far away before mankind
Before the dinosaurs, no ages survive
suffering duality.

The youth is gone, a spider crawling
into a black hole, unable to spin its web
The hope – bad blood, I think closing
my eyes was the worst mistake.

Title of My Heart

I dip this quill in ink
feeling it poke my heart
the moon nobly defending
the tides of love.
My mind is a book
touch the braille
feel it how it collapses
and expands.

I imagine a bridge between
the heart which speaks
and the soul which loves
the mind it cherishes.

The powerful conceptions
divide my lips untying all three
the wild caged organ, the fire
around my silhouette in the fever
of the night,

devour me lover
consume me

My mind is a book
she's in every chapter

the title of my heart is her name.

Motor Head

Of Gods and monsters, I destroy myself, rebuild myself.
I know of no ending without the beginning of a dead end.
The motor head of pain and grace ripped with hands
that have known morbid workings and bad brains
of Gods and monsters, we twist ourselves, untwist ourselves.

You have not seen through the eyes of others, nor felt
a thing close to someone's experience, we burn within
and die outward upon materials, praising the things
which make ease, the things that do not breathe
this pulse is perception, remember that of Gods and
monsters.

Give love the shaping hands of hope and imagination
for every birth there is a critic of life, a genius of light
a menace from darkness and an indifferent bastard
who is the most intelligent drunk on a late Friday night
who talks of Gods and monsters that crawl into his bed
and eat his dreams.

The paycheck isn't enough, the sky is dark and gloomy
the hookers have left their corners, it's raining this bullshit
and we go home with this defiance, "This is where I
belong?"
Yet who am I at close of day? The shelter, the seeker, lover
and the disquieting storm.

Do we live the grace of being of sin? We stretch our skin
hoping it's enough to wrap around the holy temple of
illumination.

To understand all things is a quest the motor head
cannot exhume from graves
nor are these tears' a permanent stain on a monumental
revelation that the Gods and monsters do in fact
crawl into my head and eat my dreams.

Walk Around Broken

I walk around broken
without you

imitating a rational smile
of expectance

I do it all the time,

you've left my marching
to the grave

the only way to show
how I love you intimately

on these earthly grounds

where you reach heaven

and tuck me in under the stars.

Lake Mind Quieted

What trembles in thy hand?
What tears in thine eyes?
Waterfalls springing new
ideas and wonders grand.

Youthful whims of summers ago
The older folks thought us crazy
free and naked, from changing winds
sprung briskly arrows from loves bow.

What is buried in a grave?
Once living artistry in motion.
How to be moved by oceans
those waves of heart beats
I'll never waiver.

What leaps from a faithful heart?
What steals joys from the soul?
What of sorrow in the losses?
Skipping rocks of memories
across the lake mind quieted.

What of dreams we do not recall?
of will and imagination to where
no stars fall, we're walking hand in hand
around the lake mind quieted by our love.

So I Obliged

She touched my face
She kissed me beyond lips

She said love me
so I obliged.

She said eat me up
so I obliged.

I love her simmering
And her my surrendering.

She said, you could move
mountains and free yourself

I replied, that sacrifice
would be conformity

Then she said, I love you
So I obliged.

Artwork

I will describe artwork
a particular one, made
of emotion
A wild rose tattooed
upon the heart.

Yeah, her nerves went like a hurricane
tornado eyes spun a web of passions
a force within herself, she quivered
and my world rocked.

A wild rose tattooed upon her spirit
sparks of cravings burst out of wounds,
this pounding, pounding of my heart
against its glass cage but never shatters.

I cannot tame myself though I'd like
to wear a mask and hide a while
the wild rose won't allow it

for she tattooed it upon my heart.

Speak Soul

Speak soul;
of the sorrows undertow
of the scents which brought
the ghost back to the heart
and why with white knuckles tight
you clutch the frame with desperation.

Speak soul;
of the joyous wonders
Dreamed child only too quick
to get here. Neither assurances
or promises quench the thirst
to pound the ground stumbling
along through heaven and hell.

Speak soul;
of memories taking solid form
as if to touch would be the last
words of a kiss, instead of the torment
that escaped your mouthed prison
the day tears burned flesh.

Speak soul;
of mysteries you have pondered,
the lands you have wandered
where your mind, heart connected
to the rivers of the sun and moon.

Speak soul;
in prayer or lack thereof
a belief, say now to someone
what ails and what soothes
the whispering pains that sullen
the dampness of depression.

Speak soul of what death cannot take;
the value of being Human.

Unfinished

The heart thwarts inconvenience;
behind the veil, that naked innocence
raw and powerful sneaks into the gaze
of your eyes - a vast refuge of expressionism
living in the artistry of how you've come through
the darkest and most tragic of deaths
to be reborn on the tongues of ravishing heart beats

My Heart to Yours

My heart, it can be scary. This unknown which crept in
however, cannot be rid of the passion.

My heart, how you have magnetized it to reach for your soul,
through the melancholia thick and heavy.

My heart to yours, I know the bruises, and the wounds
may I nestle against you with all the love within me?

Why? Because it is all I know, all I can offer, and everything
I am.

Revolutionary

Revolutionary lips connect and hypnotize,
what is said is unheard, what is done is
unhinged from the chains of passions,
with whispering fingers plunging yearning
into the mind to taste the marrow on the tongue,
two bodies lacing miraculous revelations of mysticism,
flesh upon flesh.

Sink those prevalent sensations into the undulating oceans,
riveted by the complexities we become mythological to each
other, mighty Gods of one another's soul.

Rebellious towards time we turn and bend, your
voluptuous breathing seizes my pain caressing the angst
into submission.
Crusading through the lucidity of touch
I'm an astral projection, you're the spirit
of my soul.

You're revolutionary to my living, pulling the hell out
discovering love is purely unconditional, you taste divine
and love so wildly in the euphoric state of becoming one.

I Am Cold My Love

I am cold my love
in the endless soul
searching refuge
forever expanding
the universe holds
no other angel.
I am cold my love
frozen and burst
into stardust.

Your feet upon earth delicate
You wandering nature curiously
your intelligence gathering information
the heart and soul meet somewhere
between the dust I've become
I am cold my love.

Your complexion never changes.
The silk weaving's left behind
everything you touch with such care
The curve of your smile becomes
a galaxy of shapes and pretty colors.

Frozen and burst into stardust
I fly with the wind on the paths
you walk, all that warms me
is the sunshine of your Being.

She Said

She said
dreams
are fading
whispers,
they turn
to scars
and whimper,
wishing
what could
have been
was a never was.
The world
inside broke
and I take
every chunk
of it,
love them all
until I'm out of breath.

Shadows of Today

It is the old song to cherish,
the rusted heart which can
still claim its solitude, while
beating like a wild beast
Foaming out its death
Unheralded.

The fingers clasp old frames
Breaking time into fragments
Something that went missing
found in the softer eyes of now.
Come repeat and replay

a moving history of wishes
gone wayward with the scent
of your body crashing into me.
Star after star burning passion
The flames of memory engulfing
the shadows of today.

The Tailor

It could be a he or a she.
It's made either way,
The neck tie is grief hanging low.
The collar perfectly comfortable
That is acceptance.
The pants seam just snug
The length just unnoticeably off,
They are rules of character to some
And others they are classifications
Of soul.
You will be seen and perceived
as your hair, as your eyes, as your
skin, as your climatic self, few wish
to poke you with the pins to see
what you are made of.
Shined shoes to dollar store beat
the street bummers,
They matter to the tailor.
Sunken in cheeks, bags to be checked
in under the eyes, thinning hair,
The broken thing you've become
is perfect for the tailor.
You might be fixable, living up to
economy and standards,
Manageable and tweaked, you may
make a better door stop or office clerk.
It doesn't really matter, the measurements
are taken without any care of who we really are.

We Watched the Sun Die

We were there in her room,
last confessions sucked into the gut.
Nothing last in that forever, holding her
hand quietly, where she disappears
without notice or warrant, deaths tolling
closer, we watched the sun die – together.

I find it strange how what I feel is a cause
either a man becomes hard or this pierces
that hardness breaking what makes sense.
In slow moments after her eyes closed
I imagined my pulse becoming hers
my mind living within that dark finality,
what truth can I now speak?
That some losses are actually lost
in the moment.

We watch the sun die because
we're too afraid of hearts and
too stubborn with ego's.
Lay down weapons for love
breach hate with peace
she will come back to me
when I honor her in memory,
as I watch the sun die, through
the darkness she is the light
running towards me.

See Below My Sky

Her body pure, fine and ripe
tangerine succulent dripping
off my chin,

her essences see below my sky
as I rise to meet her lips

chest heaving in awe of this
experience

the thirst on her breath
born in her body

mutilating what I thought
love making was.

The vibrations between us
twist reality with fantasy
mingling in the waters
of a fountain offering pure
enlightenment.

By The Eroded Shore

Broken dreams by the eroded shore
taken into the storied sea.
Without glory endless ghost walk the waters
whispering lullaby's once wished with the
saddest eyes known to mankind.

They fade into silent frowns, empty hands
reach out in mourning.
When they breathe in, the ripples of water
are glimmerings of what life could have been.

The moon light cast their shadows deeply
beneath the weeping of melancholy sighs
objecting to the sinking of innocence.
The sights hold no colored form, filtering
through the blackness of their wailing.
A form of self in dismay has become home
along the eroded shore.

I watch them mysteriously seeking myself
within the woe of their ghostly shadows,
the density of their somber movements surreal.
I see the depths spitting up my broken dreams.
I find myself walking on the water's surface
sobbing, "but I wasn't done with them yet."

Love

Sweetly, you never made mortal wounds
Are scars wombs awaiting your rebirth?
Who shall warm a heart, and stay, and
consist of you unconditionally?
This is the offering of substantial worth
If it were easy, would it be so worthwhile?
Honey, you hold a candle flame, passing
through the chambers where secrets whimper.
Baby girl, this shall be my strength, to be steadfast
honoring your noble purpose,
For this is life's everlasting will, and with
sacrifice comes meaning,
Not to define love, but become its breath
Within you is why I love you.

Flower Girl

A Lily flower in her hair
Freckles upon her face
Windows to mesmerizing places.
Butterfly gypsy soul
sun dressed my dreams.
She came with a going smile
and polished glowing halo.
Her words cut through the cruelty.
Her kisses I ate, her caresses I pawned
for this is a fate she'd rather sweat out
in the coverings of our skin, soft
and forgiving, carving tender meat
for the soul's bittersweet dew drops
left on our lust wasn't enough for the
lovers in the garden of passion and thorns.

Bleeding Out

The chaos
          arose
                    some thunderstorm ago.

If you choose to
               go away
                         my dearest rain
after the sun
               I will go into the fray
                         among the broken.
Fuck despair,
          I walk with my tragedy
                         in this war
for sound and soul.

The melancholy came
                    with letters whispered
into the breaths of time
                    tracing the esophagus
the fabrics seething,
               dismantling,
                         I still carry them
on burnt fingertips.

If you choose to go away
                    love of my souls' life,
let these veins rip
               wide open,
                         bleeding out butterflies
and feeding the ground
                    a sea
                         of my endless seeds.

Nowhere

Have you looked toward the dusk and wondered why
the mist swallows the scene?
Beyond anything obvious why is this rush so imminent?
There is nowhere to go
but where everyone else wants you to be.
Let's drag along the bottom of the wallet
Into the couches, behind the pillows
for the change you wish, for who you ought to have been
The one as a child you imagined, tall, rich, handsome,
With a piece of ass that would bang you all night long,
Yeah go into that mist head first diving off that building
The impact will let you know you are alive with nowhere
else to go but back home in front of the complacent brain -
washer.

Let Me Rock

Let me rock with your permission
with the whispers of your gracious
hope.
I have curled up knees to chin
without a prayer
except a feeling that your saturating
of me, may excavate my wonders from
the dark abyss.

Let me rock with your permission
to the rhythm of your ecstatic body.
I am an alter ego of my fears, releasing
how I love you at your altar.

I live in an inquisitive mind frame
let me rock back and forth with
your heart, helping me breathe.

It is the power you hold to grant me
strength, with that irresistible
resuscitating kiss.

Not as We Appear

There is a ghost in your kiss.
Your hands alive with memories,
I feel them crawling, escaping
your throat for the nails they are.
Who pulled who closer? Whose
hell is burning through illumination?
We are not as we appear, in the clutches
of greatness comes realization – the more
I ask the questions, the more I wish
you were a blur

Until

Your lips melt like butter saying a prayer
Your beautiful heart doesn't deserve to pay this price
for the ghost it keeps, nor that hard-edged noose you tie.
The bullets in that gun are meaningless
They taste like sins, and now they tremble with all those
thoughts, your weeping soul doesn't need these.

I am with you, until I am old, and my earth crumbles.

 When the negative people speak, tell them
"You take advantage of my emotions
when you dismiss them."

Look in the mirror, one eye sees the past, the other
the here and now, close them, place your hand over your
heart, I am with you, until I am old, until my earth crumbles.

You can collapse into my arms
Listen, feel, a body of hope loves
your presence, I'm sorry for the evil
doers that dwell in charming skins
but they can never define the lover
your heart holds, and I implore you
please put down the sharp devices.

Stay with us, wrapped in warmth
I love you all, I am with you
Until I am old, until my earth crumbles.

Her Winter Photograph

Like winter....but warmer
I'm denying...she's dying
bitter taste....stain linings
These bindings...too haste
One last....desperate kiss
My confessions...sucked into
dry air....I'm trying
holding on....silence steals
last words.....death mingles
skin tingles....eyes denying

As I try to bring her back to life
by pulling her through a photograph.
The resolutions fragmented, my thoughts
dissolved, my weakened knees try to stand
trying to bring her back to life.

Like darkness...dirt covers
once lovers....shadows shiver
by grave.....under moon
Godspeed...all to soon
My admissions...heard here
Past decisions...made clear
like hearing....worn breaths
dead skin...lucid tears
worn dresses...lovers soul
here's your...winter photograph

His Heart

They were born underneath the stars
an undulating cradle of black mass
cupped and swayed with them
until the cries found the light
in the center of His heart.
They breathed with purpose
still engaging the expansion
they twinkled and some burst
which begged to question what
is non-existence if life has touched
the immeasurable?
No surface is safe from the end
nobody is entitled to its eternity -
safe the soul underneath
the stars, higher than the tall dead trees
more vibrant burning out, until the ghost
retrieve their regrets, that is how not to live - no, you
be free among the giants by living how you were born
crying until you found the light in the center of His heart.

The Last

All else ends, moment after moment
The last of taste leaves its mark.

Calmly rest with my bones old friend.
Write me with your eyes, my biography.

Where once I laughed and cried, seeing
the last place where you stood,

now a shadow grows tall, I feel regrets
burn in my throat

and love chiming in my heart, the sweetest
of you still vibrantly coveting my dreams.

All else ends, but I am the moon always
watching over you.

Why Do We Wish

He plays rhythm and blues
a rusted can in front of him.
His song isn't desperate
nor about pity

it's about God and unity.
For a moment as my quarter
fell, that rusted can looked
like a wishing well

full of wars, souls, and tears
of wishes wished before,

His song is about why do we wish
when we can do.

A Cold December Day

Records indicate dear poet that on a cold December day
you went out wandering looking for the frozen river bend.
You can look here; oh you don't need to see these forms.
They're just for my amusement really, although this is rather
serious.

It says you have been looking for all of your life, and on this
morning with iced tear's and wasted blood through veins
you've gone down, struggling and oh my look at you
turning all blue, barely breathing, why do you fight so hard?

Those storms in your heart will soon come to a dead stop,
The key inside of you will be forever lost. Though I can
admire your determination, and as you fade into the other
world, I must wonder of the words you have died to say.
Yes, dear poet, it certainly is a cold December day.

Touch Me

Touch me in a way
that confesses sins.

Hold my heart to
the candle light

come kiss me with
the reality of your flesh.

Crawl through my
sexual playground
I'll slither through
your fantasies.

Touch me, kill
with your fuck
me now look into
my hell yes eyes.

No laws shall rule
how passion plays

sweating until we smell
like lust,

mind numbing
raging
yearning
building

exploring skin
fingering ecstasy

I taste your flowing
satisfaction,

touch me.

Trace

Trace this breathless kiss.
If time could freeze or
be still for a deeper penetrating
power, to compel my lips to seal
but still feel the transparency of
passions places.
Take a leap into the sea of love
you know my soul better than most.
Knowledge seizes that of heart and soul
this winsome world of your coverings.
My wondering dance in your arms.
Terms of every richness of touch
and consumption endear these moments
we are fragile glass to every current.
I can write your transformation from
their dissolves, then the mixtures you've
blended into me.
We trace time at edges and futures
Endurance's grace is how you leave me
and redeem my hearts contention.

Let Me Love You

Her fingers are feathers
turning to dust.
Her eyes are dreams
fading fast.
Her feet are moving
time is burning up.
Her heart is beating
the drums of memories.
She crumbled when we cuddled,
let me love you.

She's Like Rain

She is like rain;
you cannot gather enough of her
in the palms of your hands
You cannot swallow enough of her
to quench your thirst.
Some call those clouds, the storm is coming
but I call it the insightful gathering of puddles
of life and memories, the delicate waters
come down, and sometimes they fall hard on her,
don't try and gather them in the palms of your hands
help release her like the rain on a sunny day.

Where You Are

Where you are behind the smile
is of concern to me.
What you feel behind the laughter
is what I wish you to express.
Your drifting eyes give away
the truer inner self.
Tell me darling of these things
the reality beyond the smoke,
step through and show me your fears
I will listen faithfully and hold them
to my heart, so I may learn to communicate
more effectively with your soul.

Pools

Her eyes – deep pools.
The hearts ripples
the warmest ever felt.
The cold sleeps with her in mind
what a sincere voice – caring for the echoes
of what I could touch.
So many things to say with the softest tones of love
a symphony playing throughout dreams.
I constantly miss her, she's my best inspiration
and heartfelt smile.
She's the complex wonders of what I feel.
She is the mind that turns me on,
the one love, there is a universe inside
this precious woman and I want her to know
how beautiful she makes me feel about myself.
She is courage, creative, humble and humorous.
she is beauty as she is, there is nothing more magnetic.

Leap

I leap
and have
no wings.
There is
no miracle
no defense
against this
gravity
and I keep
falling
....falling
The powerful
velocity
executes
its fear
tearing through
wind, slicing
through prayer,
falling
...falling
As soundless
as folding hands
into one last breath
there is no miracle
no defense against
this gravity,
Falling
...falling
Until the hard
Earth bust
every bone,
and the voice
chokes on
its own blood.

Gone

Twisting a bullet of fate between fingers
until the form fits the chamber;
gone.

Sharpening a screw to the temple
This outlast the idea of sleep and death;
gone.

The walls which close in without mercy
spin the chamber, count some blessings;
they could be gone in the echoing seconds.

Then again, this is already a mess
Let's paint the madness then I'll be
gone.

Mystery

I lay near suffering to ease the grip on you.
I see the sorrows drip from love me now eyes.
All of this complexity compels the languages
of intangibles, to be constant and content.
Even in the shadows closer skin, you hurt, I ache
wishing to dream again that within tremulous tears
there are more worthwhile whims.

No matter those wishes never granted
they may be of fools who forgot to dream
or blew out candles too blind to see
the parallel blur of fault and blame.
I see the sorrows drip from love me now eyes,

They contain myself – you hurt
I ache to be a discovered
mystery.

Some of Us Will Never Know

She was as hurt as the scar cut twice
She didn't care if the water croaked, the ghost
in their bubbling forms she popped with laughter.
The same shame that broke torso from dress
fingers from ecstasy dissolve in the loathing.

When brutality meets maliciousness, her lips
no bluer and her eyes no longer bruised
that breath of dismayed clarity flushes out falsehoods
while your face still smiles and shrieks through hallowed
halls of the nightmares you built so skillfully.

Some of us will never know the strength it takes
to swallow the eulogies of the inflictions of pain
by hands, by words, by feet, by teeth kicked in
for not having supper done at five p.m. precise.

Sometimes in mid-day there are earthquakes
Where her core is hot and molten, distilled
from the reality of shopping for food or whether
She will be ready for him when he gets home
But the aisle says number eight, its baked goods
And she remembers she can make a new soufflé now.

The Devils Hand

Inhaled chaos.
Exhaled a ghostly grief
Digesting it would be too much.
A dark euphoria wanders
about this dreadful panic, it churns
in the stomachs gutter and rises
through, conquering the senses.

Sweating out depressions corrosion
of things that creep in. The slumber
is over and I beg you dear, tie your
merciful strings around my insecurities.
Play a lullaby to soften the devils hand.
Cover me as you will, a frantic lover

begging for this creatures' demise.
A ripping in two, sew it up at the seams
even though I'll speak in tongues.
Why you haven't plunged a knife
into me is a wonder of its own disturbance.

You next there, with enlightened words
Though I be obscene, you believe a power
will seek to cleanse the absurdity of this madness.
It is not within my hands to wield evil weapons.
You search that cross, unmask the red eyed hell

'You swallow needlessly upon the altar,' I spit out.
This creeping recedes to lend you my method,
A war you've waged for a conjuring of premise,
'I'm sorry Father, I let it in to execute the moral of the story.'

Tender and Endless

The young dead brain spinning in my falling tears
Woven in the mysterious grief like his changing form
Cut short too soon.

Come rage, come craft a masterpiece no greater
Than his existence, but larger than his small hands
And louder than his sullen weeping through the night.

The young dead brain spinning in my falling tears
A train wreck of misery befallen on a grave dug fresh
By deaths awful vividness, the face of beauty tangled
with the gentleness of his spirit.

Come anger, come for the bullets of heavy iron retreating
down the memories that still the air, I breathe in burst
of this deafening silence in his infancy cut too short.

The young dead brain spinning in my falling tears
Took root at his birth, the branches I imagine
would have grown to the sky, imagining and hoping
to be as tall as the sky, tender and endless.

Avenue of Hope

A tragedy within her stages a play
on the days where the light halts
its resonance. That further away galaxy
is hers, mind your distinctions with humility,
she's on the one-way street of no escaping pain.

You'll be burning on ice, if you reckon
with the illogical ego. You'll build a wall
you cannot tear down. It is her interpretation
you must paint and find the avenue of hope
to guide her to.

Your focus with patience is a vital organ
letting her know how you feel with gently
flowing currents. She is a butterfly coming
to terms as best she knows, within her cocoon
trying to break out, into the freedom of your love.

Her Breaths

She has said the seas are wild
somewhat deadly in a way, like
hands that break the fragility
of the waters gentleness.
She has kind eyes to say such a thing
as remembrances kisses where
nothing falls away.
I deny abstract notions, though lingering
towards oblivion as I trace her lips
and yet again find myself conquered.
Have you yet to run out of ways to consume me?
or are these universal waves wishing us to collide.

Trail of Serenity

On a trail of sound serenity
she falls in love with butterflies
and bees, how they glide, fly and float
milling around without a care.
She sees the birds in the trees
nature makes sounds that sing
the wonder of her vision.
She falls in love with the little things
the blades of grass
the flowers in bloom
the blue sky reborn.

She notices me smiling and chuckling
"Why are you smiling?"
"Watching you tender to this place
is whimsical and I'm listening and learning."
She falls in love with Autumn and the leaves
change to colors of her imagination.
The wind switches directions at the closing
of her eyes, she may be reminiscing in a moment
of clarity.

I'm listening and learning, her mind is more provocative
in her life philosophies, in her humming voice of a searching
for why I'm so captivated by her.

She says with a playful smile, "I'm a tigress at times."
"Darling, sometimes I'm a wolf."

She falls in love with the butterflies and bees,
the birds in the trees
the blades of grass
the flowers in bloom
the blue sky reborn

My heart beats ever so gently listening and learning.

Falling for You

I have fears, a few
the heights I may
fall from,
The ocean pulling me down
violently
Until the water in my lungs
no longer matters

I think scars are rendered with error-
The ill intended weave that fucking charm
and disguise fault as the laying blame

I stand against them, stubbornly,
Where can I reach to unearth
your significance and worth?
Good men should die for the value
not the credit.

The rib-cage shelters the heart
it fails the emotional riddles
some have manipulated
and left the afterwards,

But they too were left licking wounds
Sour and full of their disdain, if you can
hurt someone so beautiful, you are capable
of losing yourself in the madness you make.

I have fears
The heights I may fall from
but even that does not fail love
from blooming
For the heart is full of lyrics
That fit the song of your soul
The love inside my heart
devotes itself to holding
you sacred.

Ever Flowing

I can imagine through the ways you move me, the ink ever flowing.

The pen an instrument, words my symphony dancing in our kisses.

I can imagine you're tired of hearing me speak of love, but my heart is ever flowing.

My eyes as light streams, God have mercy, you're a lover's dream girl.

In awe and amazement thoughts in my mind of love making through poetry

The voice from your intellect teasing the pornography in my head.

I can imagine the embers in your mind being enflamed with a poets blowing love,

And I swear as I live and breathe It will be ever flowing, with every heart beat I write gently and lovingly in your brilliant sky.

Of Mortal Men

Where I have wept, I have carried your love.
See like full tulips, the exposed death
of things has a vivid color as continuing life unfolds.

When I could not dream in sleep and shuddered
awkwardly towards a distance out of reach
You did not recoil, but embraced me with your care.

When I could no longer speak, your angelic halo
wrapped me warmly, my strength fleeing as I
lay in the garden of the life I had lived

Sweetheart, you made the years even more worthwhile
Of mortal men I did my best to bestow upon you,
the equality of what you sacrificed and gave.

Should you love again, love him with more devotion,
With all you consist of, for death shall teach us, what is
fleeting, is worth all our heart and soul while its full
of aliveness.

My Brother

My brother, I saw the arrow strike
the mighty of the city falling.
The strong went down to their knees
and the weak arose with a roar,
Some exclaiming the revolution!
But I saw differently the eager tone
in your eyes to divide hatred and twist
off its ugly head, exposing the central
nerve as a swallowing and digesting of
individuality.

Self-Exploring

I wander into the shadows among the wailing of the wicked.
They make men's blood curdle, turning light into shades of
fear.
How far down the windy spidery tree lined road must I go?
With no heaven in sight, no clue as to what this search is
Carrying strength in the cowering faith of my heart, O God
You must be with me.

The air is dense with regrets, mangled parts of man betrayed.
You breathe in and the stench glues to your nose and throat.
Finally, a beastly man appears before a shadowed door,
I request of him, "What is this hellish place?"
Enraged he replies, "You have yet journeyed far enough."

This could be a world of the outcast, of the inhumane, or
The nature we created while consuming all we could gather.
I study a silver light ahead, my feet aching for some rest
A man in silhouette with the eyes of loneliness deep gray.
He quietly sings without words making sense, the sadness
Of self-exploring life, where it now dwells.

I say to him, "Please sir, what is this wicked dreaded place?"
Woefully he says, "I am of you as you are of me, this is
the ruins of your heart."

The Rain

Tell me, does the rain know teardrops?
Is each splash a broken thought?
Is every puddle a place to walk through?
We know the waters and what we drag
up are the whims and sorrows of the downpour.

Tell me, does the rain know heartache?
Why does it fall without complaint?
Why does it make us want to sit
by the window and watch the sums accumulate?

I sit pondering the meanings of many answers.
I hear the sounds against the leaves, rooftops
the draining gutters and the flooding of rivers,
all of this just flowing in its rhythm.

Then I imagine you blowing steam away
from your coffee cup, those full lips of my
desires smiling, it is a wonderland

a vacation from the rain.

Let's Dance

Darling let's dance in the arms of the devil
and show him the translucent God of saints
and sinners.
We'll lean into his ears and whisper
'Watch us kiss while you hiss, deception.'
To hell with the ideology of innocence
I like towing raw lines and pleasures
that steam mirrors and break the logic
of the body.

Darling let us run with chances that few get
it might be interesting in a sweet kind of cool
heart driven willingness to comprehend where
the waters get murky and our hearts drown in
one another.
A rebellion - our desires wish to twist the thorns
of blood and we'll fuck like animals in love with
this freedom.

I Love You

She picks a flower
purple and blue
and chokes it
until it weeps,
confesses
"I love you
now allow me to
pluck the thorns
from the hands
of your heart."

Labyrinth

I have seen beauty and have trembled
in awe of its exquisite life, I have feared
to touch it, for it may have destroyed me.

I've found the heart doesn't disqualify
the levels of love, it has made me bold
and brazen,

fully lustful.

The attraction is overwhelming, she's
larger than life in an abstract labyrinth
which leads to her, behind the cage

that was built to protect some innocence
that no one could sacrifice for, or believe
she deserves to keep it,

they never get close enough to steal it
because they are transparent and she
is cautiously guarded.

I will walk through fire, and acidic waters
to reach this beauty, so I may show her
my temple has been formed for her touch
and I was born to love her.

To Keep My World Warm

The alleys smell like slaughtered swine
and wasted dreams.

The sky leaps open to praise the scars
lacing the eyes with some ridiculous hope.

Escaping into the scents of cinnamon
and her lavender breath

I cave in, she takes me in chopped up
ground into her blessing of abandonment.

After brutal sex like origami limbs
leaving the feet curled and tingling

it's off to piss again from the ledge
of certain madness, where darkness
promises its emergence

but every time I return to her
she is there to keep my world warm.

Underneath

I have seen the emptiness
in these eyes

outlined by the prequels.

The windows of that soul
draped with tender shades
of life.

The eyelashes of time I think
blinking

and underneath there is a perception
what makes beauty so tangible

is the honest complexion of humanity
staring out from that emptiness.

My whispering across these seas
I confess a sultry wanting of you.

I have seen the emptiness of those
eyes so many times, my heart calls your name
sweetly

press your ears against my heart
exploring the reaches of infinite desire

this fire blazing
we both hold matches.

Morning Sex

Sunlight
and refuge.
You smirk
your naked silhouette
slips away with one
glance back.
Running water
I can still feel
your lips impressions.
A strand of your hair
plucked from a pillow
I think about the rising steam
who knew walls were meant to shake.
A scent of rain after morning sex
and aftershave.
Coffee brewing.
Settling bones
The power of your womanhood.
Everything is covered up
in playful smiles.
Your ravishing beauty hits me instantly.
Conversation, the day's work ahead.
Philosophical dreams of attainments
verses the mundane daily grind.
The glimpse I get as you sip from your mug
great morning sex and the caviar
is you sitting across from me.

As Lovers Do

Come to me and wrap
your wreathe of pain
around my neck.

I cannot carry it
but walk beside you
for the distance

We will tell these burdens
they can take things, they
can have their time

but our dedication remains
through darkness, to dream
as lovers do.

We will go by burning bridges
and the Northern Star to where
ever our hearts map us out, and
the off road ghost who once we knew
who once made us hurt will be no more
but empty nuances

to remind us how when our souls
met our scars, we made love
as lovers do, with intense veins
flowing the birth of life.

Filthy Sun and Dusty Moon

Hope dangled in
pardon the interruption
and do you have the time?
your wispy lips spoke
filthy sun and dusty moon
wayward stroking clock
towards the oceans brims
of your eyes,

the sunset from a far window
looks pale and unused
your words fall away resounding
in the silence of dying crickets
echoing in the long sought dreams
of afterwards or maybe's song.

Reality comes and sways between
the backbone of the naked soul
honey fingers along the curves
sweet tongued melody arching
the lyrics of seductive interpretations

all adrift from where we started
the ending of promise

left such a fire in the belly.

Longing You

What words can fill a page;
longing you.

How much rain can fall
from the sky;
longing you.

How long can clouds
cover the sun;
longing you.

A heart beating
and stopping
a pause;
longing you.

How many songs
come to ears;
of longing you.

There is no mystery
the earth never stops;
longing you.

How many adjectives exist
that shake verbs loose;
I am longing you.

Endless sunrises
infinite moon rises
I am longing you.

After All

The mind refrains from thinking
the death of I. The body speaks
of passing time, the horizons we have seen,
the mountains we have climbed.
After all, the flesh and bone
must rest and spirits be released.

So what is left after all is said and done?

Unfinished love, thoughts we never shared
The emotions we've left drowning
without ever flourishing, all of these after
thoughts fading in the distance.

This is the fate of life and breath
Desire and devotion to keep close
To the heart all that we covet.

After all we are born in different skins
And of different faiths.
I smile in amazement, I grieve for the lives
torn apart.

It is appealing to trace the steps we have taken.
We wear our imperfections as we should
After all it fits the kaleidoscope of the world.

Breached

Dying of yearning
in the sultry of your kiss.
Leaving levitation in riddles
lowering like your hair
how intensely lovely you can be

as I remember how your eyes dance
and how they wonder off afar
from civilization.
I've often thought, where has she
gone?

What gestures could make the brushing
back of your shadows seem so delicate
We'd be lovers in thunderstorms
and spent rainbows invisible to the naked
eye.

Oh the command you hold, to be breached
like chaos in the summoning of your rapture.

Seduction

Passion wasn't born to be tamed
it was made for the six senses
use it all when love in its most
sacred intention is calling.

Her hair covering dreams
Her eyes spinning seductions
web,

the scent from her body alluring
the sultry curves, I'm mentally
stimulated by what she'll do,

I lick my imagination, she smirks
"Come love me everywhere and
make me flow like a bursting dam."

Leave Me

Leave me sweaty and converged
with your weeping willow
bowing against the winds.

Leave me sweet letters unwritten
in the movements of your body
breaking my very limit.

Leave me a bottle of red wine
with the kiss of your fingers
unsealing broken promises.

Leave me drunk and packed
with the intensity surging
through sexy hell bent eyes.

Leave me enthralled between
your thighs and hypnotic admissions
of innocence and guilt.

Sizzle

Your words sizzle
leaving the thoughts
renderings dripping down
the souls throat.

The euphoric melancholy
is like dead tulips blooming
Thunderstorms while amidst
a cemetery for the living (the world
makes sense through your verse)

An umbrella keeping the rain
from soaking into the angst

The heavy weights are anchored enough-
I am enthralled with your echoing soul
speaking

in light of woe and love.

There is nothing more beautiful
than the individual self –

Her Words to Man

Do you detest these lips
for challenging the character
of your manhood?
When your lies slide off
the palette and into
the gutters of betrayal
do you ache and wince?
No, you call us bitches
because integrity isn't
for sale and you are cheap
and easy to please.
When you are with your girl
do you dream of my kisses?
Swish them around your mouth
like a fine aged wine?
Darling, you cannot handle it all,
your bravery is a tease for a lustful
tryst, and I require a man who can
keep his hands full of me and his mind
enticing me,
my heart is strong like a motherland,
my passion ferocious, you cannot levitate
the ghost I have known.
You lick the flames and
run like a scolded dog, that's
a modus operandi of players
You're not that slick thinking
with your prick.
Sometimes our wicked smile
will play, don't be afraid to be
bitten, it's obvious your ego needs
a woman of lethal caliber.

Into The Grey

1.

I have seen ghost light up cigarettes in the dark
They speak," I know you remember us,"
then disappear.

I look at emotions with stitches
They're real and from long ago,
I sleep on broken broom sticks
From sweeping up the glass of busted
windows.

2.

Into the grey I discover killers
and saviors of saints and sinners
some wearing coats made of thorns
others the afflictions of rose colored tears.

I find not one to idolize, but many suffering
I offer my hand, I wish to know them
God is willing, and I myself a sinner
wish they'd understand, not all is lost
in the chaos, my eyes are not saintly.

3.

You're my hero is not a pedestal
But the blooming petals of how
Beautiful you make me feel.

4.

Into the grey is where my heart
Finds its adrenaline beating
Through the foliage of your imagination,
God I'd grab you without hesitation
Drinking the blood of melancholy

Where the tears tread, her pain I feel,
They like to speak, "I know you remember us,"
then evaporate.

5.

I love her therefore I accept her as she is.
We paint rainbows with affections flight
I don't need shades, I'm not afraid
to go into the grey to show and tell
her.

Sarah's Heart Strings Symphony

This will play Sarah's Heart Strings Symphony,
 in the tune of celestial, conducted by the moon.

The stars are not twinkling, they are
playing drums against the sky.
The wind is whistling with the hum
of birds, the ocean waves are plush with harmony
The Moon strums a heart-shaped harp
with light and love.

O woes of soul, and scars of history-
let these rest on the side of worn
Bless weariness with strength
playing hope in the smiles of solace-
This galaxy, is yours, and I - Moon
conduct Sarah's' Heart Strings Symphony.
Warmth investigates what can go cold
but the sun enlightens the charming senses,
Breath and vision, body and soul.

Blinking eyes are cymbals, eyelashes
are brushes painting dreams
Closeness caressing fears, a beautiful
aching playing on these heart strings-

The raindrops are colonies of verse
settled to fall and gather in puddles-
Reflections - reach into one and find another.

Serene is the atmosphere of love
A carousel around the universe
Ravishing eyes to gaze into time
 life's full of contradictions and wonders
Humming Sarah's Heart Strings Symphony.

Violins

This is not where the sun sets or rises.
Too far into the abyss of what once was
a life without these creeping suspense's.
They form faces I can no longer see
but shape what I had known to be alive.

This pain and lonely aches are violins
playing through tiny speakers, reaching
my miniature ears on the giant weight
of my self-deceptions.

Defeat becomes such a vulgar word
but it's the winning I know in a place
that stales like the damp basement
holding me still in its static definitive.

A smile eases my disappearance
from the bones which have chewed
on the deposits of labored bitterness.
I want it good, too good
more than I wished for.

Wells of Want

I die another day without
the womb of her love.
My reborn eyes starve
for the flesh to have no end.

Every sentence could be an adjective
but I like verbs that slide inside her.
These orgasms from the chasms of the soul

euphoria is nothing without pronunciations.

Buried in my bones an ancient passion with
secret languages spoken in six bottomless
wells of want.

Empty Jar Heart

So long ago it seems I loved
with my empty jar heart
spun in cobwebs, now ancient
in a tomb surrounded by
the waterfall of tears.

There used to be no hollow
echoes or voided eyes to see
love and hope the illusion
of need.

Now I hold my empty jar heart
like an urn, I despise its meaning

as I spread the contents on
deaths doorstep.

Damaged Doesn't Mean Dead

Damaged doesn't mean dead.
There is a rolling thunder inside,
Something you have missed is alive.
Let no one bury you beneath their rubble.
To those who have manipulated the innocence
Just listen, wounded does not equal dying
She gave my heart a spinal tap, the love of
God refilled my spirit.

Sometimes in the angst as thick as oil crawling
down our throats when we swallow, we question
this breathing thing, the bleeding scars, the rewinding
nightmares. We wonder why this existence sticks to us.
I tell you this, there is a rolling thunder inside of you
Something sharp and clever inside of you is alive
Damaged doesn't mean dead.

Head Stone

Unmarked I think, no date

not even my name

just an insurmountable

feeling in quotations

"All he wanted was to love the girl."

My Winters Aching

My winters aching, insatiable red heat
softer marching off of a rainbow.
After the laughter in my darkness subsides,
the under belly is a scar in the portrait of your face.
This requiem for the moonlight, I have adored
its dagger through the rich blood of waters
Leaving my tears, a golden waterfall of
what they cannot take in order to rule the world.

The Evolution

The sight of you, a moving spiritual
experience, the evolution of passions
which scintillate the heart.
These embers ablaze, the fires of hunger
mouths become satellites
hands explore temptation
the union molding soul's desires.

I am submissive at your altar
your kiss is;
evolving need into appetite
want into cravings of flesh,
the fervor and friction, the bones
the licking, the teasing, the tension
all playing

Your being is the evolution
of my wanting;
herein it shall be pure

for your love is the evolution
of my understanding
when passions quake beneath lust
pure love magnifies its meaning.

Eternal Springs

She returns to me these notions;
Hopes eternal springs.
I am smitten with a fluttering heart.
A plethora of days gone by, finding the way
closer to the richness of a connection
that leans into me, and I cannot explain how
comforting that enlightenment is, a warm world
pulls the eye lashes open, not for a wish nor a dream
but to awaken the inspiration, and life's due wholeness.
I see her natural body, and its captivating me.

Where Your Soul Meets My Bones

Electrically charged,
condition of the skin,
Tantalized mind, scintillating my eyes
With the quotations yet said
You are the nutrients of my smile,
The adrenaline rush of love,
My veins euphoric, where the soul
meets the bone's.
And I feel as one immortal myth
Come to life.
You become the hearts motivations
And a man's courage
You make walking easier
The hazel ball in your eyes
Gazing up to some whimsical fabled moon
You are the love endeared
Where the soul meets the bones
Sweet words explore me!
Lips part,
Seas of verse
The heart knows, thus I know
Of body and spirit
Charming and determined
You are where the soul meets my bones
as a star to a million painted on the sky
I see your star shines brightly
I am in love with your energy that flows
through a continuum of self and mind,
You are where my soul meets my bones.
I'm inspired, I'm motivated,
You help me learn how to be
a better man.

Sweating

Lovers
scars dripping tears,

your intense kiss spiraling through gravity.

Lovers
sweating ovations of ecstasy,

your fragile heart roars its hunger.

Lovers
dancing in the moonlit forms of silhouettes,

your caress creating a man through your devouring

let's move into our togetherness until we collapse
like stars.

Lovers
letting oceans part

Lovers
keeping treasures between lips

and licking the temptations

dew.

Run Warm Through Us

Your eyes riddle my fever
to a pitch perfect temperature
There is an endless desire to
create movements and muscles
that leave skin moaning and hearts
throbbing.
Mount world of body – five orgasms
short of sunlight.
The soul of the moon absorbed
in your breathing
drawn into your wanting intensity
electricity convulses the grip
high off your sensual ecstasy
I taste, the thrill of these spices
chap my lips.
Run warm through us, the after pleasure
of fingers locking, one fathomless kiss
to fill the pours of love.

A Walk Among the Stars

There is a magic to your blinking
thoughts dancing around the wondrous
flourishing of forever in the heavenly atmosphere.

There is a miracle in the senses we've become use to.
So busy to notice the song of the rivers before us
their melodies flowing with the natural beauty of
their forms.

You cling to me with the vital air of mystery
which begins to question the paths I follow
"A walk among the stars," is her offering.

The moon looms overhead like a guardian
of our midnight dreaming hearts, we ask
not about secrets or dangers for our lips
seal no fate but our kiss promises hope
is not lost.

Tenderly the earth provides a magnificent
aura of possibility and she leans into me
to whisper, "When your strength is soft
I'm seduced by the power of your heart."

Her infinite graciousness held in such
reverence by the galaxy I take in
it doesn't just pronounce the feelings
It generates goodwill and unconditional love.

Darling

Well darling it is windy enough to tear the eyes
into recollections puddles of wonders.
How it went right, how it went wrong.
Why doesn't it fit? Where did the time go?
Where's my smile? Where's my better tomorrow?

I don't exactly know what to say
by God's grace tomorrow will have a revealing face.
How beautifully strength reminds us to carry a torch
of hope.

You have uncovered a golden device throughout
the years, it's the aura of your heart, a halo of silver linings
A method to expose more of human compassion.

Your eyes win the day of my sight, I see the past pains
and into days afterwards I stay steadfast to let you know
I think the world of you, and if it pours on you, I will open
an umbrella of love made with my spirit, have faith we will
rise into the days to come.

Pleasures

Ten centuries it feels the soul has lived.
A fountain of youth to wonder in lands
of skin and bones, yours of course
adaptable to moods and delivery.

A frenzy builds upon the desire
to warm fires between lips
executing the perfect honey
drop into insanity.

I still not surrender to your sugar coatings
but peel layer after layer, the soul of these
fruits between us, lust for love the hearts harvest

which leads to pleasures and songs of sex
in a physical altered state of pandemonium
your body a canvas perfect with its reactions
we delve deeper into the volume of pleasures.

With What You Feel

Let me massage your breast
not with words or ideas
of a lustful tongue,

but with heavens hand, gazing deeply
into the eyes of your honesty.

For I breathed life once before
and upon a dream
of your perfect body.

Some suggest the tampered heart
has a temper;

be wild in my arms
insecure in my head
but come with what you feel

like a hurricane
or falling feather

I will love you gently.

Promiser

Promiser, you hold up these tears
On what Gods honor do you offer
these dissolving prayers?

Promiser, you've been kissing shoes
with that demons' tongue despising
virtues,

O promiser you cut me dry, with a vile
curiosity drinking my life of blood
Sucking my own thoughts into

into the crevices of madness, I'm
impaled by your breath, right through
me runs the glory.

O promiser, sinister betrayer of the heart
On whose integrity do you swear the lies?
When eyes disappear into the twisted
shadows of the dead,

do you glare at the stars and find them reborn?

O promiser, anger trying to tear down
the sky as she broke the mirror and a
thousand selves screamed "This is not
the way away from home."

O promiser, you whisper in the pilgrims
voice so sweetly after the crimson runs,
you hold up these tears, on which Gods
altar do you offer your life for the places
you should not have tread?

Paint

They probably want more fire
Passion, hot metaphors for fucking.
They should know my heart is drying
It pumps out paint
A satin finish
And it's dark, yeah
As dark as oblivion,
It's dense
enough to paint
a mansion, no, a
Madhouse,
Where the rubber
Walls melt and all
My friends inside my head
Are broken out, bleeding
From my nose, sucking
in wind through my mouth
To quicken the drying of my heart.

So Close Together

Your fatal kiss
kills solitude.
It whispers
Longings, long
after dreams.
Your kiss
slays solitude,
Your caressing
eyes invade the heart
working through my veins,
the pulse it rushes,
at the soulful stroking
of your miracle-hands.
Your fatal kiss drives
through me, awakening
a source of passion
never to be matched,
shaking the world
and finding ourselves
whispering longings
our souls have craved
to connect to our hearts.
Our kiss
kills solitude,
Hands together
Finding our secret selves
leaning so close together
they're in one eternal embrace
which quickens the pulse
to lovers of all things
you and I share.

Salt

Let the world fall away baby
Just like a dreams adaptation
of the breathing things that sting.
Let's pluck the devils horns from
one another's wounds.

Make our souls taste sweet and unwind
with sly clever looks, "It's alright sweetheart
the moon has arisen, nothing can drive it
out of the saturation of your presence."

It lights for you to cast out shadows of doubt
My heart is trustworthy, strong with its faith
Let's lick the salt from each other's body, until
we are entangled together, consumed
spent, to be reborn at dawn.

The Compelling

The swaying of emotions,
tidal waves to a quiet sea,
unbelievable the size of everything.
We've reached to smash
We've sought to love
We've ravaged in pain
We've experienced many
different versions of ourselves.
Outside sources, inside voices
parallels and paradoxes, it
makes me wonder, are we
universes in a mirror
beyond comprehensible
reflection?
This is sensationally
riveting,
Why love with so much heart?
Why hate with equal strength?
Why serve yourself criticisms
that others say?
We look so vague sometimes
we lose humanity
to the threads of what has been
done unto us.
I've seen a man love
And I know it's me in the
shallow waters observing
this little world,
We'll feel a million things
before we're done;
The echoes and the whispers
of past and present
which drives the heart
to seek and hope.
I love you, which is the
compelling within me
and a weapon against
the darkness.

How I Wreck Myself

May we wake up between the thighs
alarm clocks
        and find the warm sun
                  glistening
off of everything that has perplexed
and complicated the vices
of our souls.

Drip riddles out of our bodies until
all wrongs and poor choices
              seem so long ago
and sink into some abyss

where we are lost and found through
touch and sound.

May my hands become a flesh memory system
for how divine you feel against my skin
and my mouth the same of how sweet
you taste.

Things that linger in the air I'm daring
and convinced,
           sew me to your bones.

The conversations of your mind
to your heart
        what do they say about me?

Oh how I wreck myself with yearning passion.

Still Frames

God, I want you
every blink is a wishful
glimpse of soul, its aching's.

The hour glass flows
age develops these
still frames of love
and devotion.

You become that presence
sitting next to me – adoration
rendering me into heart beats.

Darling, sweet loving kept
in the chemistry between us.
With every breath you take
root in my senses, and these
still frames speak from my being

God, I love you.

The Soul Tree

I've heard of a place,
with a grand lit meadow
Where every purpose meets
all wishes like unveiling secrets.

I shall search for it, and if I find it
before you do, I will wait, until history
is prevalent and I am old.

Should eyes greet every wonder,
then all kind gestures possessed by
souls giving nature, will find deliverance
 in ultimate devotion.

Meet me by the old soul tree
where our lives will connect
Under the simmering magic
of the moon lit night.

Keep devoted eyes
in the promises
of swept over hearts,
take me under the old soul tree
and whisper your fears
into the vault of love,

Keep faithful the heart
when we embrace,
the roots will strengthen
there will be no doubt
The sunshine is a labor of sacrifice.

The defining ages come
In this moment when
You can gather every atom
Of me in your gaze, orbiting
The old soul tree, above the moon
and stars align, and I'll speak like

forever pouring out of me;

What you love, I shall care for.
What you seek, I will help
you find.
What you treasure, I shall protect.
What you say, I shall soak in.
How you smile and how you laugh
enlighten my soul, the life of my heart.

What you endear to, I shall ask and learn,
under the simmering magic of the Moon,
how and why, love never dies.

A Beautiful Creation

You can be mired in the after hours,
When the day has ruled the mind
rest in the quiet winds of time.
We will wrong the good intentions,
and try like hell to right them.

Whatever mess was made of grace
it's not always the end of possibility.
The shadows of deaths grip broken
by the constant hope we breathe
into one another, like bees to honey.

I sing you from my soul, by far
the deepest root within this continuum.
You are a beautiful creation worth every ounce
of the heart, squeeze me dry only to fill again
with love.

Sweet Things I Have Never Known

Her smile while sipping coffee
or her lips blowing steam away,
the wishes in her daydreaming eyes
sweet things I have never known.

Her comforting touch in the coldest hours
Her whispering while she sleeps underneath
the ageless aching of a souls' content.

It may be they are nameless, but the colors
have painted a fruitful tree made of sweet
things I have never known.

No imagination renders conclusions useless
her fingers turning pages, her heart questioning
reasons, the sigh that out last hours, they could be

sweet things I have never known
but concluded on my own merit
admissions that I love her so deeply
my tears hug me offering their comfort.

When the clock is all I can hear
I wonder of, the sweet things
I have never known.

Gaze

Listen to the silences intensity
Building up to its climatic burst.
Proof and truth are abstract
In your contradicting roar.
End the war between attention
And release.

I want neither bars or cages to
inhabit your harmonious rapturing.
Be free I implore you – magnificent
gentile, tarnished, and glorious.

You radiate through the cold steel
of time – ageless in my gaze,
heaven breathing earth back
into the body as you move me
spiritually.

The Requiem

These star lit passions
which have been pursued
are burning.
There is a season within
man that never changes;

He of purest heart
can love.

A harp,
A note, constant
In its tone,

Adrenaline love runs
through these veins.

My almighty,
this tide is you
love…

I'm not knotted
by waves of havens sake,
sacrifice means giving
beyond flaws and means,

we're perfect in the harmony
of waters which have never
been able to drown us.

May I be a sinner?
Yes.

At last confession
my body craves your hunger
And my soul desires
You!

The Lying Life Inside

What comes so heavily?
The lying life inside.

Baby, come rest your head
of worry on my heart
No fear of whatever comes apart.
When our kisses are broken
love will make sense of them.

What comes so quickly?
The lying life inside.

I've heard what's been done
to you, the brash singularity
of a wrecking ball once known
as a charming man.

I cannot tell you how to wander in
your own mind, how to turn around
The corners of those emotional mazes
Or how to ride those roller coasters,
I can only prove I'm here to be with you.

I only know the lying life inside
Is a deception, and I will dive
into those dark waters with you
We can learn not to hurry, but
To keep ourselves together

What comes to life?
How you feel in my arms
Safe, protected, and on my life
that is honor.

Your Blood

Your blood leads towards this disaster.
You said, "Drive these nails in deeper."
The company was for sale without debt.
They didn't wear ties, they didn't care
about scars.

Your blood comes closer to forgiveness.
You said, "Drive these nails in deeper."
So some eager trolls decided to eat the forest.
they decided tigers should be on a list
it's like a system going out of stock.

They mocked the rib cage, ate a woman
and a brother murdered a brother without
the mentioning of hell, but what they
really need

are the nails to be driven deeper
into consciousness.

Profound

If you've ever felt
your life hasn't been
profound,
I've come to tell you
otherwise.
You unleashed my heart
and these feelings still
bleed through the veil
cry through the mask
come through the soul
to the words I write,
sometimes they even lullaby
me to sleep.
You've given birth.
You've beaten cancer.
You've given hope when
dreaming was impossible.
The love and fight within
is a growing tree, with roots
of inspiration and the foliage
of the aura of your soul.
For all the tears you have
ever cried, I wish to place
my heart within you, soaking
up whatever is left of them.
Always - a promise I intend to keep
To honor, to cherish who you are,
I fell hard for you, and I still feel it
Every waking day – to bed you, is my
Dreaming soul, to love you is profound.

www.ingramcontent.com/pod-product-compliance
Lightning Source LLC
Chambersburg PA
CBHW031321040426
42443CB00005B/178

* 9 7 8 0 6 9 2 6 3 9 7 4 0 *